Animal Engineers
BIRD NESTS

by Stacy Tornio

FOCUS
READERS

FOCUS READERS

www.focusreaders.com

Focus Readers is distributed by North Star Editions:
sales@northstareditions.com | 888-417-0195

Produced for Focus Readers by Red Line Editorial.

Photographs ©: Stacey Ann Alberts/Shutterstock Images, cover, 1; Red ivory/Shutterstock Images, 4–5; Paul Reeves Photography/Shutterstock Images, 6; Efimova Anna/Shutterstock Images, 8–9; Vinicius Bacarin/Shutterstock Images, 10; Tracy Kerestesh/Shutterstock Images, 12; Craig Hanson/Shutterstock Images, 14–15; Ge stock/Shutterstock Images, 17; old apple/Shutterstock Images, 18, 29; Marcel van Os/Shutterstock Images, 20–21; Alexander Sviridov/Shutterstock Images, 22–23; trabantos/Shutterstock Images, 25; Glass and Nature/Shutterstock Images, 27

ISBN
978-1-63517-859-3 (hardcover)
978-1-63517-960-6 (paperback)
978-1-64185-163-3 (ebook pdf)
978-1-64185-062-9 (hosted ebook)

Library of Congress Control Number: 2018931109

Printed in the United States of America
Mankato, MN
May, 2018

About the Author

Stacy Tornio is a children's writer in Milwaukee, Wisconsin, and the author of *Bird Brainiacs*. She is the former editor of the magazine *Birds & Blooms*, and she loves birds—especially owls, woodpeckers, kingfishers, and hummingbirds.

TABLE OF CONTENTS

CHAPTER 1

NESTING SEASON

The sun is rising. But the birds are already hard at work. They gather twigs and bits of grass. The birds will use them to make nests.

Early spring is nesting season. The birds look for a place to **breed**.

 Some birds use moss to build their nests.

▷ **A bald eagle cares for its chicks in a large nest.**

A nest provides a safe place for them to lay eggs.

Bird nests can be found in many places. Some birds make nests on the ground. Other birds build nests high in trees. Some birds even use holes in trunks or stumps.

Nests come in many shapes and sizes, too. An eagle's nest is big and messy. A hummingbird's nest is tiny and neat. No two nests look the same. But all nests are an important part of a bird's **life cycle**.

FUN FACT

An eagle's nest can weigh more than 4,000 pounds (1,800 kg).

CHAPTER 2

BUILDING A NEST

Birds use their beaks to build their nests. First, they pick up nesting material. Then they carry it to their nesting spot. Birds may hold the material with their feet. They add one piece to the nest at a time.

 A weaver twists palm leaves together to make its nest.

▷ **An ovenbird makes its nest from clay.**

Birds weave the pieces together.

This makes the nest strong. Birds

use many materials to make their nests. These include grass, twigs, and leaves. Others build with mud, fur, or feathers. They might even use paper or yarn.

Female birds usually do most of the work to build the nest. But sometimes the males will help.

FUN FACT

A few birds do not build nests. For example, the killdeer lays its eggs on the ground.

▷ **Baby hummingbirds sit in a nest on a tree branch.**

Many nests are round. This shape is known as a cupped nest. American robins build cupped nests from mud and grass. Hummingbirds build cupped nests, too. They may cover the nests with moss or **lichen**.

Some even use spiderwebs to hold the nests together.

Many birds make nests in bushes or trees. They build their nests where branches join together. Large birds such as eagles and owls make bigger, messier nests. These nests are often high up in trees. But some owls make nests among rocks.

FUN FACT

A hummingbird egg is approximately the size of a pea.

CHAPTER 3

RAISING BABIES

A mother bird lays eggs in her nest. Then she sits on them for several days. This time is known as the incubation period. The bird might sit through rain, wind, or snow. So, the nest must be strong.

An osprey collects materials for its nest.

Eggs are fragile. They can break easily. So, birds tend not to make nests out in the open. Instead, their nests are often hidden in trees. This helps protect the nests from the weather. Many nests use **camouflage**, too. These nests are hard to find. This helps protect the baby birds from **predators**.

Baby birds are small and weak. But they wiggle. Nests are woven to be strong. They will not break apart when the babies move.

Baby birds cannot fly, so they must stay in the nest.

Baby birds stay in the nest for several days after hatching. The mother and father birds come to check on them. They bring food for the babies to eat.

A black drongo brings an insect for its chicks to eat.

Eventually, the babies leave the nest. The nest might be used again. The mother bird might lay more eggs there. Or another bird might use it.

Each **species** of bird takes a different amount of time to make a nest. An American robin spends five to seven days building its nest. Then the mother bird lays eggs. She sits on the eggs for 12 to 14 days. Then they hatch. The baby birds leave the nest 14 to 16 days after hatching.

FUN FACT

Eagles use the same nest year after year.

WOODPECKERS

Unlike many birds, woodpeckers do not weave nests. Instead, they carve out holes in trees. The holes are called cavity nests. Some woodpeckers make round holes. Others make holes shaped like a rectangle.

To make a nest, a woodpecker pounds on the tree with its sharp bill. Drilling into trees is hard work. So, woodpeckers look for dead or **decaying** trees. These trees have hard outer wood. But deeper inside, the trees are soft or **hollow**. This makes it easier for the bird to drill a hole.

A woodpecker can hit a tree up to 20 times in one second.

CHAPTER 4

LEARNING FROM BIRDS

Scientists can learn many things by studying bird nests. Birds choose nesting spots carefully. They need trees for protection. They need plants for food. They need lakes and rivers for water.

 Cormorants make nests near Lake Ontario in Canada.

Bird nests can be signs that a **habitat** is a good home for other animals, too. Sometimes birds stop building nests in an area. This can show that there's a problem, such as **pollution**. Other animals may be in danger.

Sometimes bird nests cause problems. Birds might make nests

FUN FACT

Scientists who study birds are called ornithologists.

 Sometimes storks build nests on top of houses.

on or inside buildings. Woodpeckers can damage trees when they drill holes. Other species take leaves off trees to build their nests. This can hurt the trees.

However, bird nests can also help the land around them. For instance, birds help spread seeds. Birds carry plant material when they build their nests. As birds move the material, they drop seeds along the way. New flowers and trees grow where the seeds fall.

Birds build nests all over the world. The nests can be many shapes and sizes. Each one is an important part of nature.

A baya weaver's nest hangs down from a tree.

FOCUS ON
BIRD NESTS

Write your answers on a separate piece of paper.

1. Write a sentence that describes why birds build nests.

2. Do you think eggs would be safer in a cupped nest or in a hole in a tree? Why?

3. Where do woodpeckers lay their eggs?
- A. in cupped nests
- B. in holes in trees
- C. on the ground

4. Why might other animals be in danger in an area where there are no longer bird nests?
- A. The problems that caused the birds to leave may affect other animals, too.
- B. The birds will no longer be around to warn the animals if a predator is coming.
- C. The animals will not be able to eat the shells that drop from the bird nests.

5. What does **materials** mean in this book?

*Birds use many **materials** to make their nests. These include grass, twigs, and leaves.*

- **A.** objects used to build something
- **B.** parts of a bird's body
- **C.** pieces that have been taken apart

6. What does **fragile** mean in this book?

*Eggs are **fragile**. They can break easily.*

- **A.** heavy and hard to move
- **B.** common or easy to find
- **C.** not very strong

Answer key on page 32.

GLOSSARY

breed
To have babies.

camouflage
Colors that make an animal difficult to see in the area around it.

decaying
Rotting or breaking down.

habitat
The type of place where plants or animals normally grow or live.

hollow
Having an empty space inside.

lichen
A plant-like material made of algae and fungus.

life cycle
The description of an animal's life from beginning to end.

pollution
Harmful substances that collect in the air, water, or soil.

predators
Animals that hunt other animals for food.

species
A group of animals or plants that are similar.

TO LEARN MORE

BOOKS

Harrison, George H. *Bird Watching for Kids: Bite-Sized Learning & Backyard Projects*. Minocqua, WI: Willow Creek Press, 2015.

Hughes, Catherine D. *Little Kids First Big Books of Birds*. Washington, DC: National Geographic Kids, 2016.

Tornio, Stacy. *Bird Brainiacs*. Apex, NC: Cornell Lab Publishing Group, 2016.

NOTE TO EDUCATORS

Visit **www.focusreaders.com** to find lesson plans, activities, links, and other resources related to this title.

INDEX

Answer Key: 1. Answers will vary; **2.** Answers will vary; **3.** B; **4.** A; **5.** A; **6.** C